02/91

NOSTRADAMUS
The Future Foretold

Edited and Translated by
Dan Hofstadter

Illustrated by
Paula Goodman

Peter Pauper Press, Inc.
WHITE PLAINS • NEW YORK

Introduction

Michel de Nostredame, or Nostradamus as he is usually called from the Latinized version of his name, was born in 1503 and died in 1566. He was, and remains, a puzzle.

Because Nostradamus was supposed to have had prophetic powers, one might think that he must have been a wild-eyed magician, but nothing could be further from the truth. In fact, Nostradamus was an upper middle-class doctor, a general practitioner and responsible family man who lived in the Town of Salon, in Provence. He had a medical degree from the highly respected School of Medicine of the University of Montpellier, and had made his reputation fighting epidemics, which were then common in the south of France.

The evidence we have suggests that Nostradamus took the part of empirical investigation against the remnants of medieval superstition. He was against bleeding, for example. He believed in the contagious nature of certain diseases then often thought to be forms of possession or divine retribution. And he seems to have suspected that the earth revolves around the sun!

How, then, did this man of science start predicting what would come to pass? We must remember that Provence in the sixteenth century was still underpopulated because of the mass extermination of the Albigensian "heretics," that it was subject to erosion and flood, threatened by the feuding of Catholics and Huguenots, and decimated by contagions borne by the *siroc* or southeast wind; in short, it was a land of terrible insecurities. Nostradamus was a kindhearted man, and he wanted to help his countrymen gain a certain insight into the future. He began by issuing almanacs for farmers, and presently discovered, from the fulfillment of certain minor prognostications, that he seemed able to predict certain events. Then, if we credit the story, he correctly foretold the death of King Henri II, the death of his eldest son François, and the betrothal of his younger son Charles. These astonishing prophecies made him a favorite of that great intriguer, Catherine de' Medici, and he has remained the posthumous favorite of French princes, prelates, and politicians to this day. His fame has spread all over Europe and to the United States.

In reading Nostradamus' prophecies, which he arrived at primarily by clairvoyancy (possibly with a little help from astrology, then as now a branch of occult learning much consulted by highly placed French people), we notice certain concerns — feudal warfare, plagues, famines, religious bigotry, and floods. Naturally many of his predictions have to do with such things, and deal with what was for him the near future. Nostradamus was nationalistic, Catholic, and rather liberal-minded, and wanted to put his countrymen on the right course — rather like a Renaissance political commentator, a Walter Lippmann of old Provence. But other of his prophecies are darker and more confused, and see farther into the future; some are very broad and foretell remote events.

Most of Nostradamus' predictions have not come true, or at least not yet. But just enough very specific ones have been fulfilled to unsettle even the staunchest skeptics. A startling example is his prophecy that a Frenchman of the Bourbon dynasty would one day rule over a kingdom called "Etruria" (the Latin name for Tuscany). In 1801, Napoleon created just such a country, and placed Louis of Bourbon-Parma on the throne. This case (and many others like it) may of course be a coincidence, or perhaps Napoleon and other great agents of history knew about Nostradamus and wanted to fulfill his predictions — which wouldn't of course make them any less remarkable. In any event, even the absolute unbeliever will enjoy finding historical episodes that eerily fit what the prophet foretold.

Nostradamus presented the greater part of his predictions in a collection called "The Centuries." This title does not refer to periods of time but to the work's arrangement, which consists of cycles of one hundred quatrains each. Though the quatrains rhyme according to several schemes, Nostradamus was no poet, and he did not follow the rules of Renaissance French prosody beyond this rather rudimentary level. He also ignored the laws of grammar, putting verbs in the infinitive — like a speaker of pidgin — as often as in the future tense. The result is that some of his prophecies have a timeless, oracular quality. Many phrases observe no set word-order, rather as in Latin, but since the nouns and adjectives lack the case-endings of Latin words, the author's sense is often obscure.

Obscurity, in fact, is the hallmark of these prognostications. They are written in sixteenth-century (essentially modern) French, but since Nostradamus was a southerner, Provencal words are occasionally used. There are also many vestiges of old French, and some low Latin (and a few Greek) words. In translating the prophecies, the author's basic sense or meaning in each quatrain was first determined as a key to obscure words and phrases. Rhyme, on the whole, has been dispensed with, though rhymes or slant rhymes have been left where they happened to occur in the translation.

Nostradamus can be enjoyed for the puzzles he has left for us to solve, and for the sound of his words and the power of his images. Possible meanings are suggested (some by the translator, some by the publisher) after many of the quatrains, but take care as you enter this mysterious world!

D. H.

Nostradamus

I. 1

Seated at night in secret absorption,
Reposing alone on the stool of brass,
I see a flame flare out of the darkness
That helps me foretell what will come to
    pass.

[*Nostradamus as he prophesies*]

I. 3

A litter overturned by a whirlwind,
Faces covered with cloaks — then upstarts
Beset the republic, topsy-turvy
Fall the judgments of the Red and the
    White.

[*Reign of terror/Robespierre?*]

I. 17

For forty years no rainbow will be seen:
For forty years it will be daily seen:
The parched earth growing drier and drier,
When it shines it will shine through a
    deluge.

[*Famine and drought*]

I. 21

Needlessly troubled, they will not dare touch
The white slime that deep down feeds the
  bedrock
And oozes forth milky from the chasm —
They do not know that earth is only clay.

I. 25

Lost, found, hidden for ages and ages,
The shepherd is praised as a demigod:
But before the moon ends its great cycle,
He will be dishonored by other winds.

[*"Pasteur" translated as "shepherd."*
  Could it be Louis Pasteur?]

I. 27

In Guyenne's soil, under the blasted oak
Or thereabouts, is the treasure hidden
That was gathered for so many long years:
Its finder will die blinded by a spring.

[*Finding of a tomb?*]

I. 30

A stormy sea, a strange ship, an unknown
Port. The vessel putting in, heedless, blind
To palm-branches signalling in the wind.
Death, then pillage: too late the alarm.

[*France's loss of Algeria?*]

I. 32

The mighty empire will soon be reduced
To a little place that will one day grow,
A very lowly place in a mean land,
Where he shall come to lay down his sceptre.

[*Shrinking of the Holy Roman Empire?*]

I. 34

Before the French prepare their defenses,
A bird of prey flies on the left-hand side:
One thinks it bodes well, one ill, one neither,
But the weak party holds it a good sign.

[*Kaiser or Hitler invading France?*]

I. 35

In a single combat, on a battlefield,
The young lion will overcome the old:
In a gilded cage he'll put out his eyes,
Two wounds made one. Death follows, most
  cruel.

[*Henri II's death in Nostradamus' lifetime*]

I. 41

City besieged, and assaulted by night:
Few survivors: fighting hard by the sea:
A harlot fainting at her son's return:
Poison and letters hidden in the fold.

[*Harlot-Vichy France? De Gaulle her son?*]

I. 44

In brief: sacrifices shall be resumed,
Transgressors shall be put to martyrdom,
No more abbots, friars, or novices,
And honey shall be much dearer than wax.

[*Abolition of worship of God during
  French Revolution?*]

I. 45

The founder of sects hurts his accuser:
The beast in the theater, the masque
    prepared:
The sage ennobled by the ancient deed:
By sects the world confused and divided.

[*Religious conflict as source of war?*]

I. 57

In great dissension the earth will tremble:
Harmony, broken, will lift its head high:
The mouth will swim in its blood: on the
    ground,
The face anointed with milk and honey.

[*Execution of Louis XVI? Pearl Harbor?
    Nuclear war?*]

I. 60

An emperor is born near Italy
Who will cost his empire a dreadful price:
They will say that even his own henchmen
Will consider him more butcher than prince.

[*Napoleon!*]

I. 65

The handless child's first sight of fierce
     lightning:
On the tennis court, the princeling wounded:
A crag split, thunderbolts starting to grind:
Under the oaks, three trussed up round the
waist.

[*Observe present-day royal families to see if this
     occurs*]

I. 67

The great famine that I feel approaching
Will bide awhile, then spread across the
     world,
So long and cruel that men will grub for roots
In the woods, and tear infants from the
     breast.

[*Worldwide hunger*]

I. 82

When the columns of wood begin to quake
And redden with chalk blown by the south
     wind,
Then a great assembly will rush outdoors,
Dismaying Vienna and Austria.

[*Reunification of Italy?*]

I. 85

The king disturbed by the lady's reply,
Ambassadors will despise their own lives:
The great one will counterfeit his brothers:
Two will destroy hate, envy and anger.

[*Said to be murder of Duke de Guise by Henri III*]

I. 86

The great queen, when she sees herself
  vanquished,
Will outrun any masculine courage:
Naked, on horseback, she'll ford the river,
By iron pursued, betraying her faith.

[*Marie Antoinette? Mary Queen of Scots?*]

I. 95

Before the priory a twin is found,
Of monkish blood both ancient and heroic,
Whose renown will so grow in the order
That folk will remark upon his breeding.

[*Man in the Iron Mask?*]

I.86.

I. 96

Though charged to raze the temples, and
    pull down
All heresies, perversions of the faith,
He'll hurt the stones more than the living
    souls,
Lulled by a dulcet dinning in his ear.

[*Counter-Reformation?*]

I. 97

What fire and sword did not know how to
    do,
The honeyed tongue in councils shall
    achieve:
In sleep and dreams the King shall meditate
And no more wish to bleed his foes to death.

[*King dreams of impending death?*]

II. 4

From Monaco to Sicily the coast
Shall be desolate: no city or town,
Outside or inside its walls, shall withstand
The barbarian depradations.

[*Mussolini seizes Provence in 1940?*]

II. 8

Temples hallowed in the old Roman way
Shall no more be built on rude foundations:
They shall take more humane and pristine
  laws,
And expel most of the cults of the saints.

[*Counter-Reformation?*]

II. 9

For nine peaceful years the lean one shall
  rule,
Before he succumbs to a bloody thirst:
For him a great race without faith or law
Shall be murdered, though by a far gayer
  man.

[*Seems specific and therefore perhaps hasn't yet
  occurred*]

II. 12

Closed eyes opened by an ancient fancy,
Of friars' cassocks he shall rid the world:
Yes, the great king will chastise their frenzy,
And plunder their gold through the priory
  gate.

[*Vague — an anti-religious movement?*]

II. 13

The soulless body sacrificed no more,
The day of dying changed to a birthday,
The Divine Spirit will delight the soul,
Baring the Word in its eternity.

[*Judgment Day?*]

II. 20

Brothers and sisters, captured far and wide,
Will find themselves passing before the king,
Who will gaze upon them with steady eyes,
Vexed with their markings on nose, brow
　　and chin.

[*African slave-trade?*]

II. 23

The palace bird driven out by a bird
Almost as soon as the prince has arrived:
The foes are repulsed beyond the river,
But there they resort to the feathered shaft.

[*Notice bird/feathered image*]

II. 29

The man of the east shall depart his seat
And cross the Appenines to visit France:
Piercing the heavens, the rain and the snow,
He shall strike all the people with his rod.

[Attack from the Orient — by air?
  USSR overrunning Western Europe?]

II. 31

In Campagna the Volturno shall swell
Till the meadows are covered with water:
Both before the long downpour and after
You will see nothing green but the treetops.

[Flood of Volturno River in Italy]

II. 36

The great prophet's letters have been seized,
Fallen into the hands of the tyrant:
Though he may try hard to defraud his lord,
He will quite soon pay for his thieving.

II. 39

One year before the Italian conflict,
Germans, Frenchmen and Spaniards man
   their forts:
The republican schoolhouse collapses
And almost all are choked in the debris.

[*Fall of Republican Spain/Mussolini occupies
   Provence?*]

II. 40

Soon afterward, without a long interval,
A tumult will be raised by land and sea:
The naval struggle will intensify:
Greater degradation by fire and beast.

[*In 1940, one French fleet scuttled in
   Toulon, the other bombed by R.A.F.?*]

II. 42

Cocks, dogs and cats will be sated with blood
From the wound of the tyrant found
   murdered:
Mangled arms and legs on another's bed
Who was not afraid of a cruel death.

[*French Revolution-Death of Robespierre?*]

II. 44

The eagle, soon pushed back into his camp,
Shall be driven away by other birds:
Then the sound of trumpets, cymbals and
  bells
Shall bring the senseless lady to her senses.

[*The Third Reich pushed out of France? Napoleon
  in retreat from Moscow?*]

II. 45

Too much the sky mourns the
  Hermaphrodite,
The newly-begotten: near the heavens
Human blood is shed: death delays rebirth
For the great race: relief comes soon and
  late.

[*Air war?*]

II. 54

The city is vexed, as the flood recedes,
By a foreign people and remote from Rome:
A handless daughter, a domain too strange,
A lord-mayor seized, city gates untried.

[*Rome attacked after a flood?*]

II. 57

Before the clash, the high wall shall crumble,
Unforeseen and lamented the great lord's
Death: born flawed, most men shall brave
    the current
Till the banks of the river grow crimson.

II. 66

The town besieged through a good omen,
The people are trapped inside the palace:
Through great perils the captive shall
    escape,
In a short time his destiny recast.

[*Hundred days of Napoleon after escape
    from Elba?*]

II. 82

Through hunger the prey shall capture the
    wolf,
The assailant soon in extremity,
With the true heir hard on the last man's
    heels,
He shall not flee from the thickening crowd.

[*Obscure*]

IV . 3I.

II. 97

Beware, Roman Pontiff, of approaching
The city wherein two rivers flow: near there
You shall spew out every drop of your blood,
And your people too, when the rose shall
    bloom.

[*Assassination of Pope in future?*]

II. 98

The one whose face is bespattered with gore
From the recently sacrificed victim —
He too must die, the augury says, die
For the Bride when Jove is in the Lion.

[*A martyrdom for the church when Jupiter is in
    Leo?*]

III. 16

With martial wishes in his angelic heart,
An English prince will pursue his fortune:
In the second duel his gall will be pierced
By one whom he hates but his mother loves.

[*Prince Andrew in a second war, after the
    Falklands?*]

III. 21

In Conca, by the Adriatic Sea,
Will appear an utterly horrid thing
With a human face and a fish's tail,
Which will be landed without line or hook.

[*What a husband for a mermaid!*]

III. 23

Ah, France, beware lest ever your vessels
Should sail beyond the Ligurian Sea,
Lest Doge and Prophet pin you in the isles,
And make you gnaw horses' and asses'
    bones.

[*Partially incorrect prediction of Trafalgar?*]

III. 24

This enterprise would cause great confusion,
Loss of men and treasure beyond counting:
No, you must not extend your grasp that far:
France, let what I say now be remembered!

[*Trafalgar again?*]

III. 44

When the animal tamed and trained by man
By great pains and efforts will start to speak,
Then the lightning will so harm the virgin
That she will be seized and hung in the air.

III. 47

The old monarch, driven out of his realm,
Goes to the East to ask for help: fearing
   crosses,
He folds his banner: to Mitylene
He will journey, over land and by sea.

[*Obscure, Mitylene is the Greek island of Lesbos*]

III. 54

One of the great ones will flee into Spain,
Whose long wound will open, and bleed and
   bleed,
And armies will thread the mountain defiles,
And ravage the country, and rule in peace.

[*Franco, the Spanish Civil War*]

III. 94

For five hundred years they will recall him
Who was the ornament of an era:
Then all at once he will beam forth great
  light,
And gladden the men of that century.

[*Nostradamus?*]

IV. 1

Behold now a measure of blood unshed:
Venice crying that succor be given,
And (after having endured for ages)
Opening her gates at the horn's first blast.

[*Venice surrenders needlessly to Napoleon*]

IV. 7

The youngest son of a detested prince
At twenty has a patch of leprosy:
Of grief his mother wastes away and dies,
And he shall die too where the loose flesh
  falls.

[*Specific and horrible, but unfulfilled*]

IV. 16

By license the free city is enslaved,
Made a haven for dissolute dreamers:
Grown from five to over five hundred score,
Since the king no longer forbids them.

[*The drug culture?*]

IV. 21

The transformation will be difficult
But city and shire will gain in the exchange:
Heartened — the knave replaced by a wise
   man —
Land, sea and people will raise their estate.

[*De Gaulle replaces Petain?*]

IV. 26

Now such a vast number of bees have
   swarmed
That nobody knows from where they have
   come:
A night ambush, a guard among the vines,
Five babblers, not naked, betray the town.

[*Napoleon's coup d'etat of 1799*]

IV. 30

Eleven times the moon rebuffs the sun,
And all are raised or humbled in degree:
What starvelings then shall stitch with
    thread-of-gold,
What secret shall the pestilence unveil?

IV. 31

The moon at midnight over the mountain
Shines only in the mind of the new sage:
His pupils implore him, "Live forever":
Body aflame, hands on chest. Noon eyes.

[*Striking imagery, but obscure*]

IV. 41

One of the weak sex, seized as a hostage,
By night will elude all the sentries:
With sly language she will deceive the chief,
And betray him, alas, to the people.

IV. 45

In a war the king will desert his realm,
His minister fail him in time of need:
Most ruined or slain, a few will survive,
And their wounds will attest to their trials.

[*Napoleon at Waterloo or Fall of France in 1940?*]

IV. 47

The fierce black one will try his bloody hand
At fire and sword and the drawing of bows:
Then his people will be greatly afraid,
Seeing men hanging by neck or feet.

[*Idi Amin?*]

IV. 52

A town beseiged, men and women on the
    walls,
Their leader on the verge of surrender:
Then a strong wind arises against the foe,
And drives him off with lime, dust and
    ashes.

[*Stalingrad?*]

IV. 53

The fugitives and exiles are recalled:
The heights are rearmed by fathers and
  sons:
The cruel father and his men lie choked:
His loathsome son wallows deep in a well.

IV. 55

For when is death foretold, the statue stained
With blood, the tyrant slain, the people
  praying
To their gods? — When caws shall rasp from
  the tower
Of brick, when seven hours the crow shall
  croak.

[*Statues do bleed, it is claimed, but meaning is
  obscure*]

IV. 56

After the triumph of the raving tongue,
The mind is tempered to tranquillity:
The winner harangues the people with blood,
Roasting the tongue and the flesh and the
  bones.

[*Moscow show-trials of the 1930s?*]

IV. 55

IV. 58

All Tuscany awash in human blood;
The sun gulped down by a greedy gullet —
His heir gone, his dame borne off to Turkey,
The lord bringing water in a bucket.

IV. 92

The head of the valiant captain cut off,
It will be thrown at the enemy's feet,
But when his corpse is hung from the
　　sailyard,
The oars, bewitched, will row into the wind.

[*The imagery foreshadows Coleridge's* Rime of
　the Ancient Mariner]

IV. 93

A serpent approaching the great royal couch
Will be spied by a lady, who hushes the
　　dogs:
To France will so royal a prince be born
That heavenly princes look down to see.

[*Birth of Duke of Bordeaux in 1820?*]

V. 4

The big mastiff, chased out of the city,
Will snarl at the unlikely alliance;
After driving the stag into the fields,
The wolf and the bear will defy each other.

[*World War II?*]

V. 5

Under the pretext of freeing the town,
Usurping its power and its people:
Egged on to outrage by the young whore's
   lie,
Betrayed in the field while reading false
   rhymes.

[*The ''false rhymes'' are surely not those of
   Nostradamus!*]

V. 7

When they find the bones of the Triumvir,
Hunting for the deep and puzzling treasure,
Then no one will cease in all the region
From digging for a lead and marble thing.

[*Triumvir probably refers to Roman leaders.
   Otherwise unclear.*]

V. 9

The great arch demolished down to its base:
The friend expected by the captive chief:
Borne of a lady of hairy forehead
And bearded face, by guile the Duke is slain.

V. 19

Great monarchs of gold augmented by
    brass;
A treaty denounced, and a war by youth
Provoked; a dead chieftain mourned by his
    tribe;
A land awash in barbarian blood.

[*Assassination of Archduke Ferdinand by
    Gavrilo Princip at Sarajevo?*]

V. 21

Following the death of the Latin king,
These things shall befall the men whom he
    helped:
A fire reflected in divided spoils,
Public death for the rash ones who risked it.

[*After death of Mussolini?*]

V. 7

V. 25

The Arab prince: Mars, Sol, Venus in Leo:
The reign of the Church succumbing by sea:
Toward Persia nearly a million men:
True Snake invades Egypt, Byzantium.

[*Middle East War in 1987?*]

V. 26

The slavish nation shall by martial luck
Be raised to preeminent power:
They shall trade their prince for a
    provincial,
And cross the sea with a highland army.

[*Soviet (Slav) penetration into Persian Gulf?*]

V. 35

For the free city on the crescent sea
(Which ever bears a stone in its belly),
The great lord's war begins: an English fleet
Coming in a fine rain to take a branch.

[*Siege of La Rochelle?*]

V. 36

Quarrelsome and deceitful, her brother
Will blend a mineral in with the dew,
Put it on cake for the slow old woman:
She dies tasting it, rustic and simple.

[*Obscure prediction from Nostradamus
the pharmacist*]

V. 39

His ancient bloodline woven by long hands,
From a true branch of the fleur-de-lys grown,
He'll cause the Florentine arms to flourish,
Lodged as heir to the Etrurian throne.

[*1801 — Napoleon founds "Etruria" and puts
Louis of Bourbon-Parma on the throne.*]

V. 45

The splendid empire shall soon be laid waste,
And whittled to a scrap near Ardennes
Wood;
Then the firstborn shall behead two bastards,
And Redbeard the Vulturine Nose shall
reign.

[*Fall of France in 1940? Vulturine Nose is
De Gaulle?*]

V. 59

Too long at Nimes the English chief tarries,
For Redbeard's relief is marching toward
     Spain:
Mars is summoned, he will soon kill many
When a bearded star will fall in Artois.

V. 66

Not far from the forsaken aqueduct,
Under the ancient vestal monuments,
The metals gleam like the sun and the moon,
The gold-embossed lamp of Trajan
     glimmers.

[*A lamp from a Temple of Diana will be
     unearthed?*]

V. 69

No longer does the lord falsely slumber,
For apprehension has replaced repose:
A phalanx of gold, blue and vermilion
Shall gnaw subject Africa to the bone.

[*Louis-Philippe / Algeria?*]

V. 73

The Church of God shall be persecuted
And her holy cathedrals violated;
The child puts out the mother in her shift,
And the Arab connives with the Pole.

V. 76

In the open air he will pitch his tent,
Not caring to dwell in the cities: not
At Aix, Carpentras, Vaucluse, Cavaillon,
Mont or Lisle: from all these towns he'll
    vanish.

[*Unclear, but towns are near Salon in Provence.*]

V. 96

With the rose in the midst of the courtiers,
And the people's blood gushing in fresh
    strife,
They shall seal their lips when speaking the
    truth,
And succor shall be too late in coming.

V. 99

Milan, Ferrara, Turin and Venice,
Capua and Brindisi shall be vexed
By the Celts — vexed by the Lion, his eagle-
Like army, when a British chief rules Rome.

[*English invasion of Italy — 1943?*]

VI. 9

In the holy temples scandals are made
Which are greeted like paeans and honors;
Strangely tormented, the great head expires,
Graven on medals of silver and gold.

[*Sins of the clergy?*]

VI. 11

Seven branches will be reduced to three:
The elder ones will be surprised by death:
The two will be seduced to fratricide:
The conspirators will die in their sleep.

[*Children of Henry II?*]

VI. 14

Far from his land he will lose the battle,
A king in flight, pursued, then taken fast,
An unschooled oaf enchained in gilded mail,
Under false garb — the enemy agape.

VI. 37

As the ancient building is completed,
Ruin falls from its roof on the great lord:
While the culprit hides in a rainy wood,
They will accuse an innocent dead man.

[*Perhaps a restoration in the future?*]

VI. 44

In Saxony, a freak, half-bear, half-sow:
With naval arts a tempest conjured up:
In the Arabian Sea a foundering fleet:
At Nantes, by night, a rainbow shining forth.

[*Crammed full of prophecies, could happen*]

VI. 61

So folded, the great carpet does not tell
Even half of its story: how, driven
Out of the realm, he seemed harsh from
    afar,
So that all believed in his violence.

VI. 69

It will not tarry long, the great sorrow,
And those who once gave will be forced to
    take:
Hungry, thirsty, in scandalous union,
They will pass naked over the mountains.

[*A general statement of life and death? More
    specifically, persecution of the clergy?*]

VI. 72

In a feigned fury of divine passion
The great master's wife will be ravished:
Then the judges, wishing to doom her creed,
Will betray her to the ignorant mob.

[*Czarina Alexandra and Rasputin?*]

VI. 74

Once exiled, she will return to the realm,
Her enemies proven conspirators:
Now more than ever her time will triumph,
And seventy-three will meet certain death.

[*Elizabeth I (but she was never exiled)? The
French Revolution?*]

VI. 93

A greedy prelate, fooled by ambition,
Will one day want too much: into the trap
He'll blunder, with all his accomplices:
He who chops wood sees all against the grain.

[*Very general, but certainly this prophecy has been
many times fulfilled!*]

VI. 100 (Variant)

Daughter of the Breeze, shield of the ailing,
Where the amphitheater is cut out
Against the sky, for you the signs bode ill:
You shall be captive, and more than four
times.

VII. 7

Above the battle of the light horsemen
The great crescent's downfall is proclaimed:
Disguised as shepherds they kill sheep at
    night,
And dark runs the crimson in the ditches.

[*A rout of the Turks?*]

VII. 8

Flee, Flora, flee the approaching Roman,
At Fiesole will battle be given:
Much blood shed, your signoria in chains,
Not a single church spared, nor a woman.

[*Flora (Florence) attacked by the Pope?*]

VII. 11

The royal child will despise his mother,
Poking at her eye and mauling her feet.
Such disrespect! Such disobedience!
Over five hundred of her people slain!

[*Louis XIII and his mother, Marie de' Medici?*]

VII. 13

The tributary city by the sea
Is captured by one with a shaven head,
Who exiles the miser, rousing his hate,
And rules like a tyrant for fourteen years.

[*Napoleon retakes Toulon?*]

VII. 25

An army so weakened by endless war
That there is no treasure for soldier's pay:
With no gold or silver they strike copper
Coins, or French brass stamped with
    crescent and throne.

[*American forces at Valley Forge?*]

VII. 38

The eldest prince, on a capering steed,
Spurs it so rudely that it bolts: oh mouth,
Mouthful, ankle howling in the embrace,
Horrible dragging and trampling to death!

[*Some possibilities in history, but Prince
    Charles beware!*]

VII. 41

The bones of the hands and the feet locked
   up,
(The house long empty, because of a noise),
Digging in dreams, shall also be dug up,
(The house healthy now, lived in without
   noise).

[*A haunted house, or possibly allegorical?*]

VII. 43 (Variant)

When two unicorns are seen, one rampant,
The other cast down, with the world
   between,
Then men will be bent to the breaking point,
And the nephew will run away laughing.

[*Loosely, US-USSR nuclear confrontation?*]

VII. 83 (Variant)

Sultry breeze, threats, weeping, timidity,
By night in bed assaulted without arms:
Ah, such calamitous brutality,
The tears unchecked, the wedding song a
   dirge.

[*Rise of divorce in Florida?*]

VIII. 1 (Variant)

Several will grow confused while waiting:
The inhabitants will not be pardoned:
Those who desire to persist in waiting
Will not be granted an hour too many.

[*Appeasement before World War II?*]

VIII. 2 (Variant)

The envoys will meet and talk about peace
In the name of powerful lords and kings,
But that peace will not so soon be at hand,
Unless they obey more than the others.

[*Chamberlain's "Peace with Honor"?*]

VIII. 3 (Variant)

Alas what fury! Alas what pity!
What pity there shall be between peoples:
Never has such cordiality been seen
As wolves share with their noses to the
    ground.

[*Soviet-Nazi Non-Aggression Pact divides up
    Poland?*]

VIII. 4 (Variant)

Many people will desire to parley
With the lords who will make war upon
    them,
But they will only be turned a deaf ear:
Alas, if God does not send peace on earth!

[*Yalta, Potsdam and the Iron Curtain*]

VIII. 5 (Variant)

Much generous aid will come from all sides
From distant peoples who want to fight back:
All at once they will find themselves hard
    pressed,
And no longer so able to assist.

[*Chiang Kai-shek?*]

VIII. 6 (Variant)

Alas, the ambition of foreign princes!
Take heed lest you let them into your land,
For that would entail terrible perils
For many countries — even for Vienna.

[*Austria lets Hitler take over?*]

VIII. 18

Come up from Florence, and cause of his
 death
A short time ago, by old wine and new,
Whom she poisons with meat she'll cure
 with fruit,
Since three white lilies have made her think
 twice.

[*Refers to a Medici princess?*]

VIII. 23

Without any signature, stamp or seal,
In the queen's own coffers, letters are found:
Then whisked away by an iron-clad hand.
Who is the lover? You will never know.

[*Intriguing scandal at Court?*]

VIII. 25

Deceitful love, stealing into a heart,
Caused a maid to be ravished in a brook:
Ah, lustful one, though you feign half a hurt,
Your father will twice sever soul from flesh.

[*Royal gore?*]

52

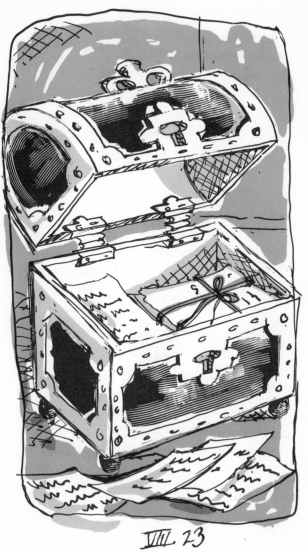

VIII 23

VIII. 28

These are the effigies, bloated with gold
And silver, which after the abduction
Were cast into the flames: far-away eyes,
What in these marble omens frets you so?

VIII. 37

The fortress commanding the Thames will
    fall
And the king be imprisoned within it:
Near the bridge, in his shirtsleeves, he
    prepares
To die: then they lead him off in fetters.

[*Charles I imprisoned in Windsor Castle?*]

VIII. 57

From footsoldier he'll rise to emperor,
And trade the short tunic for the long robe:
Valiant or worse when at grips with the
    Church,
He'll soak the priests as a sponge soaks
    water.

[*Napoleon*]

VIII. 65

The aging man, his chief hopes dashed, will
    reach
The summit of empire: for twenty months
He will rule, the cruelest of tyrants,
But he shall yield to one crueler still.

VIII. 74

The king rides so far into the new land
That the townsfolk assemble to greet him:
But he will soon prove so perfidious
That no bells will peal and no banners wave.

[*George III and the American Revolution?*]

VIII. 76

A man in England, more butcher than king,
By force will usurp the empire: lowborn,
Craven, lawless, without faith, he will bleed
The land: his time is so near that I sigh.

[*Oliver Cromwell?*]

VIII. 80

Innocent blood of widow and virgin,
Icons ablaze in a pupa of wax —
Beholding the Red One's hideous deeds,
All are dumbstruck, and by horror
    transfixed.

[*Stalin — mass murderer!*]

VIII. 82

Spare, tall, dry, playing the loyal valet,
In the end he'll have nothing but his leave:
With letters and poison in his collar,
He'll be nabbed on the way out — or will
    he?

[*The butler did it!*]

VIII. 88

A noble king comes to Sardinia
Who will hold the Kingdom only three
    years:
Careworn, jeers pursuing him into sleep,
He will join a few colors to his own.

[*King Charles Emmanuel IV of Sardinia?*]

VIII. 100

Alas for the abundance of tears shed,
From high to low and lowest to highest:
With too much faith, a gambler stakes his
  life,
While some die of abundant want of thirst.

[*Reader's choice!*]

IX. 2

"Begone all of you, on both sides!" resounds
From the Aventine hilltop: the Red Ones'
Blood alone can still such ire, Colonna
From Prato and Rimini deported.

[*Bloodshed in Italy?*]

IX. 8

The younger son, lately crowned, kills his
  sire
After a mortal and unfair combat:
The letter found, suspicions bring remorse,
But the wolf has settled in the crib.

IX. 12

Silver Hermes and silver Artemis,
Their statues will be lifted from the lake:
Though the sculptor casts about for new clay,
Both he and his will be showered with gold.

[*Buried treasure?*]

IX. 23

The youngest prince will be playing
    outdoors,
Under the arbor, when the lattice falls
On his head: with sacrificial incense
His royal father will hallow the day.

IX. 32

A long column of fine porphyry found,
Capitoline writing under its base:
Twisted hair: bones: Roman might put to
    the test:
At Mytilene a fleet astir.

[*Marble (porphyry) on Lesbos (Mytilene) but
    meaning unclear*]

IX. 34

The single part, afflicted, is mitred:
The conflict returning over the tiles:
With five hundred, he betrays, is titled:
Both Narbonne and Saulce, we have oil
    through knives.

[*Louis XVI at Varennes*]

IX. 52

From one side comes peace, from the other,
    war,
And never have they waged it so fiercely,
All over France spilling innocent blood,
Bemoaning the loss of women and men.

[*Catholics vs. Protestants?*]

IX. 65

Going into a corner of Luna,
He is captured and sent to a strange land:
The unripe fruit stirs a monstrous scandal:
And many are rebuked though one is
    praised.

[*Astronaut on moon runs into trouble?*]

X.89

IX. 78

The Greek lady of hideous beauty,
Made happy by suitors beyond counting,
Will be banished to the Hispanic realm,
Where, miserable captive, she expires.

[*Democracy (the Greek lady) starts to die in
Europe?*]

IX. 96

His troops denied entry to the city,
The Duke will enter through cunning and
wiles:
Guided in secret to its ill-manned gates,
He will sack it and murder its people.

[*Crafty Dukes often do this.*]

X. 16

Happy in his life, happy to rule France,
Knowing nothing of blood, death, or
plunder,
A king unseen, sniffing in the kitchen,
He will be envied his flattering name.

[*Louis XVIII of France?*]

X. 17

The captive queen sees her daughter grow
    pale
Because of the grief locked up in her heart,
And piteously weeps at Angoulême,
Knowing cousin shall never wed cousin.

[*Marie Antoinette and her daughter, Madame
    Royale?*]

X. 30

A nephew and blood of the saint has come
To uphold with his name both arch and vault,
And kill his foes, and banish them naked,
And change their green vestments to red and
    white.

[*Louis Napoleon perhaps?*]

X. 41

Where the burg of Caylus verges on
    Caussade,
Not far from the bottom of the valley,
You'll hear the songs drifting up from
    Villefranche,
The lutes and the zithers, and the soft strings.

[*Not a prophecy, just a description of the local
    countryside*]

X. 43

Too sweet hours and too much royal
    kindness:
Too light suspicions of a loyal wife:
Too many fortunes hastily altered:
Too great good nature will cost him his life.

[*Louis XVI?*]

X. 60

I weep for Monaco, Genoa, Nice,
Savona, Siena and Malta:
For Módena, Capua, and Pisa too,
Their blood and a sword for a New Year's
    gift.

[*Princess Grace dies, as do other rulers?*]

X. 89

The brick walls shall be replaced with marble
In seven and fifty pacific years:
Joy to mortals, the aqueduct rebuilt,
Health, rich harvest, joy, and honey-sweet
    years!

[*Years of prosperity*]

X. 100

But the great empire will be for England,
The strongest power for three hundred years,
Her armies will post over land and sea
And much discomfit the Iberians.

[*Defeat of the Spanish Armada / rise of British
Empire?*]

X. 100 (Variant)

When the fork will be held up by two stakes,
With six half-horns and six open scissors,
Then a great seigneur and heir to the toads,
Over the whole world shall gain dominion.

[*Use of roman numerals may unlock this riddle!*]

XII. 36

A fierce attack is prepared in Cyprus:
Tears in my eyes for your imminent ruin:
Both Moorish and Byzantine fleets
    destroyed:
Two different ones aground on the rocks.

[*Naval battle at Cyprus?*]